Made in the USA
Middletown, DE
04 May 2023

30021076R00071